READING
FUNDAMENTALS

by Kathy Furgang

GRADE
4

New York

New York

An Imprint of Sterling Publishing
1166 Avenue of the Americas
New York, NY 10036

ISBN 978-1-4114-7884-8

Distributed in Canada by Sterling Publishing Co., Inc.
c/o Canadian Manda Group, 165 Dufferin Street
Toronto, Ontario, Canada M6K 3H6
Distributed in the United Kingdom by GMC Distribution Services
Castle Place, 166 High Street, Lewes, East Sussex, England BN7 1XU
Distributed in Australia by Capricorn Link (Australia) Pty. Ltd.
P.O. Box 704, Windsor, NSW 2756, Australia

For information about custom editions, special sales, and premium and corporate purchases, please contact Sterling Special Sales at 800-805-5489 or specialsales@sterlingpublishing.com.

Manufactured in Canada
Lot #:
2 4 6 8 10 9 7 5 3 1
03/16

www.flashkids.com

Dear Parent,

Being able to read and understand nonfiction texts is an essential skill that ensures success not only in the classroom but also in college and beyond. Why is nonfiction reading important? For one thing, close reading of nonfiction texts helps build critical thinking skills. Another reason is that nonfiction reading builds your child's background knowledge. That means your child will already have a wealth of knowledge about various subjects to build on while progressing in school. You can feel good knowing you'll be laying the foundation for future success by ensuring that your child develops the necessary skills that nonfiction reading comprehension provides.

The activities in this book are meant for your child to be able to do on his or her own. However, you can assist your child with difficult words, ideas, and questions. Reading comprehension skills take time to develop, so patience is important. After your child has completed each activity, you can go over the answers together using the answer key provided in the back of this workbook. Provide encouragement and a sense of accomplishment to your child as you go along!

Extending reading comprehension beyond this workbook is beneficial and provides your child with the opportunity to see why this skill is so essential. You might read a newspaper article together and then discuss the main ideas. Or head to the library to find a book on your child's favorite subject. Remember, reading is fun. It opens the door to imagination!

What Is Jupiter Like?

We know that the planets in our solar system come in many shapes and sizes. But how does Jupiter compare to the size of Earth? Well, if Earth were the size of a nickel, Jupiter would be about the size of a basketball. Jupiter is the largest of the eight planets in our solar system.

Jupiter is known as a "gas giant." That's because it is made of gas instead of solid rock. The planet has a very strong magnetic field. It is needed for the planet to keep moving around the Sun. It is also needed for the planet's many moons to orbit, or move around, it.

A giant storm has been raging on Jupiter for hundreds of years! It's called the Great Red Spot. The swirling storm can be seen from space. This giant spot is even bigger than Earth!

When we explore space, we often look for signs of life. We look for places that could have supported life in the past. We have not found any evidence of that yet. Are we looking in the right places? We know living things cannot survive on Jupiter. Some life forms may be able to live on some of Jupiter's moons, however. Some of Jupiter's moons have oceans beneath their crusts! Imagine a faraway ocean that supports life. Imagine that it stays hidden in one of Jupiter's moons. What an amazing discovery that would be!

[handwritten annotations: "at least 67 moons"; "3rd"; "S U N"; "M V E M J S U N" with "Mercury Venus Earth Mars Jupiter Saturn Uranus Neptune" written vertically below each letter]

4

Complete each sentence.

1. When comparing Jupiter and Earth, the larger of the two planets is
   Jupiter.

2. Jupiter is called a "gas giant" because it is made of gas instead of
   solid rock.

3. Jupiter stays in orbit around the Sun because of its strong _[scribble]_
   magnetic field

4. Jupiter has _67 many_ moons.

5. Earth and Jupiter are similar because they both have _a moon [crossed out]_

6. The Great Red Spot on Jupiter is a storm that has lasted _for_
   hundreds of years

7. The most likely place to look for signs of life around Jupiter is
   in it's moons

8. Underneath the crust of some of Jupiter's moons are _oceans_.

Desert vs. Forest

On Earth, there are many different ecosystems. Even within a single US state, there can be big differences in the environments. California has both forests and deserts. The differences between these two ecosystems are nothing short of amazing.

Redwood Forest

The Redwood National Park in northern California is home to some of the tallest trees in the world. Some are 2,000 years old and tower 300 feet (91.4 m) above the ground. The area adds to the beauty of the California coastline. It gets plenty of rain for its rivers and streams. It is not unusual to see a mist in the air as you gaze up at the spruce and redwood trees. The forest is home to many animals. They make their homes in the trees and on the forest floor.

Mojave Desert

Like all deserts, the Mojave receives very little rain each year. Temperatures in this southern part of the state can be very harsh. One area of the desert, called Death Valley, has reached 134 degrees Fahrenheit (57 degrees C). Canyons, mountains, and mesas can be found in the Mojave. Some of the dry mountain regions cause big differences in temperatures. The higher you go in the mountains, the cooler the temperatures. The kinds of trees that grow in the Mojave, such as Joshua trees, require little water. The soils provide a home to cactus and other plants that need a dry environment.

Is there anything that both areas have in common? Both have been recognized as special regions that are protected by the California State government. When an area is protected by the state, a limited amount of building is allowed. It is preserved for people to enjoy. They can hike, camp, and visit these areas year-round.

Read each sentence. Write *true* or *false*.

1. The Redwood National Park gets the same
   average temperatures as the Mojave Desert.   _____

2. The Redwood National Park and Mojave Desert
   make up all of California's ecosystems.   _____

3. The Joshua tree grows in the Mojave Desert.   _____

4. The California state government protects
   the Redwood National Park.   _____

5. Some of the tallest trees in the world grow
   in the Redwood National Park.   _____

6. It is common to see mist in the Redwood forest.   _____

7. The hottest temperatures in the Mojave Desert
   are found in Death Valley.   _____

8. The Redwood National Park and Mojave Desert
   do not have anything in common.   _____

Ellis Island

The United States is called a "melting pot" because it accepts people from everywhere on Earth. From 1892 to 1954, more than 12 million immigrants were welcomed to the shores of the eastern United States. They entered at a center on Ellis Island. These people came from other countries to start a new life. They became part of America's population.

Ellis Island was a processing center. It kept records of the people who arrived at the nation's busiest port, the port in New York City. Most of the ships sailed to New York from Europe. The records listed the names and ages of everyone on the ship. They tracked the countries from where each person came. Physical exams were given to people to make sure they were not ill when they entered the country.

The records from Ellis Island have become part of the country's history. People today can use the records to trace exactly when their family members arrived.

Ellis Island can be spotted from miles away because the Statue of Liberty is on nearby Liberty Island. The statue stands in New York Harbor, with one arm up high, holding a torch. To Americans and immigrants alike, the statue represents freedom. It stands for the opportunities that people can have in the United States if they work hard.

People visit the buildings at Ellis Island to remember how the nation grew and changed. Ellis Island stands for the courage of its citizens. It is a reminder of the struggle of immigrants who arrived in the country generations ago and made a new life. It is a link to the country's history.

Answer the questions.

1. Why is America called a "melting pot"?

_____

2. Where is Ellis Island located and when was it in operation?

_____

3. How does the author show that Ellis Island was more than just a processing center? Underline a sentence that helped you answer the question.

_____

4. What kinds of records were taken about new immigrants when they arrived at Ellis Island?

_____

5. Where did a large number of the immigrants arriving at Ellis Island come from?

_____

6. What does the Statue of Liberty stand for?

_____

7. What does Ellis Island stand for today?

_____

8. How does Ellis Island link America to its past?

_____

How Inventors Think

What made Thomas Edison tick? What was Benjamin Franklin thinking when he invented swim fins? In many ways, inventors are just like everyone else. They use the same technologies that we use. They drive the same cars and use the same gadgets in their homes. But inventors are different from everyone else in one important way. They ask how the normal things we do every day can be improved. They ask a lot of questions about how life can be better. Then they go one step further and take action to solve problems.

For example, inventors might ask how a car can be made safer. They research car accidents. They think about what can be done to keep people in car accidents from being hurt. Then they use their knowledge of science and math to create a solution to the problem. That might mean making safer seatbelts or better air bags for cars. This is what makes inventors different from other people. They go beyond asking questions and focus on finding a solution.

You can say that inventors try to make the world a better place. Some think about the needs of people with disabilities. They try to come up with solutions for the problems these people face in their everyday lives. Others think about making daily tasks easier for people in their homes. New cooking tools or appliances are invented all the time. Life seems to get easier and easier, thanks to the original thinking of inventors.

Like everyone else, inventors find problems in the way we live every day. But they take things even further by using their skills and knowledge to solve the problem. Do you have what it takes to be an inventor?

Read each question and circle the correct answer. Then answer the questions below.

1. How are inventors different from everyone else?

a) They brainstorm ways to solve problems.   b) They research what is available.

c) They try out new ideas and materials.   d) They ask questions and take steps to solve problems.

2. Inventions that would especially help people with disabilities include _____.

a) new sources of energy   b) tools to help someone around the house

c) faster ways to get to outer space   d) computers that work faster than ever before

3. According to the passage, what makes an inventor different from other people?

a) They know exactly what people want.   b) They try to make the world better.

c) They understand how to sell new items.   d) They think cars should be safer.

4. Helpful skills the inventors use to make new products include _____.

a) sales and marketing   b) reading and writing

c) math and science   d) foreign languages

5. Most new inventions are made in hopes of _____.

a) solving problems   b) changing history

c) creating new problems   d) making money

6. What are some benefits of continuing to make new inventions for cars?

_____

7. How did Benjamin Franklin work in the same way inventors today work?

_____

8. Now summarize how inventors think differently from others.

_____

International Space Station

Where do scientists from different nations get together to research? In space! The International Space Station, or ISS, is a huge laboratory. It is also a spacecraft that stays permanently in space, about 220 miles (354 km) above Earth. It orbits, or moves around, Earth. Astronauts from different countries live on the space station and work together to find out more about outer space.

The ISS is about the size of a football field and weighs nearly a million pounds (454 metric tons). The space station has sleeping compartments for six astronauts to live on board. It is filled with laboratories for scientists from all over the world including Canada, Japan, Europe, Russia, and the United States. The first crews started living on the ISS in 2000.

There is very little gravity in space. Astronauts who live on the ISS must learn to adjust. Without gravity, they float through the ISS instead of walking. They sleep in small compartments instead of lying down on a bed. The change in gravity is difficult on the human body, so astronauts must exercise when they are in space. They use bikes, treadmills, and weight-lifting machines. These keep their muscles and bones strong.

The ISS is an important link between Earth and space. It helps us learn what it is like for people to live in space for a long time. It allows humans to look farther into space than we can from Earth. While each country or region has its own laboratories, the crews also work together. They work to keep the space station in good condition. They do repairs and keep all parts of the spacecraft working well. This often means wearing space suits and working on the outside of the spacecraft. When they come back inside, they are in their home away from home.

Draw a line to match each word from the passage to its meaning.

1. ISS
a. a place for scientific research

2. laboratory
b. a separate section of a place

3. permanently
c. the force that pulls objects toward Earth

4. astronaut
d. constantly; for all time

5. compartment
e. a spacecraft for research

6. gravity
f. an area with special traits or characteristics

7. region
g. a person who is trained to travel in space

8. Now summarize the passage.

_____

_____

_____

Dinosaurs: A Tooth Story

Fossils are the remains of plants and animals that lived millions of years ago. Dinosaur fossils are some of the most fascinating of all fossils. Why? People want to know what life was like when these ancient creatures walked Earth.

Fossils help us learn more than just what dinosaurs looked like, however. They also give clues about how the animals behaved. This includes finding out what the animals ate. Scientists may never know exactly how animals lived more than 65 million years ago. But looking at fossils can give hints. For example, different dinosaurs seem to have different tooth shapes. Scientists think that the shape of dinosaur teeth shows what the animals ate.

For example, the sharp, pointy teeth of *T. rex* show that the animal ate other animals. The shape of the teeth helped *T. rex* rip into the flesh of their prey. They used the teeth to catch and eat their meals.

The flat teeth of *Triceratops* showed that the animal likely ate plants. The flat teeth helped them bite branches and grind and tear at leaves.

With each new discovery of dinosaur fossils, we learn a little more. With each new discovery, more pieces of the puzzle are put together. For example, someday we may understand how some dinosaurs cared for their young. We may find out how long they lived. But there still may be things we never discover. For example, what color were their body coverings? What sounds did they make? Learning from fossils is a slow process. But the details are worth the wait. It's amazing how much we can even tell just by looking at the shape of a fossil tooth! Fossils are clues to the past.

Answer the questions.

1. What is the name of the remains of plants and animals that lived long ago?

_____

2. How long ago did dinosaurs live?

_____

3. How can scientists tell what dinosaurs ate?

_____

4. What kind of teeth did a dinosaur that ate meat likely have?

_____

5. What kind of teeth did the dinosaur *Triceratops* likely have?

_____

6. What other clues can scientists get from fossils?

_____

7. Give three examples of things scientists might learn about dinosaurs in the future.

_____

8. What questions do you have about dinosaurs?

_____

Giraffes

Did you know that the giraffe is the tallest living mammal on the planet? Giraffes spend the majority of their lives standing. They even sleep while standing. Baby giraffes can be so big that they are even taller than a full-grown human! They are able to stand thirty minutes after being born. They often learn to run on that same day. Some giraffes sleep a surprisingly short amount of time—as little as thirty minutes a day!

Giraffes live mainly in the African Savanna within the plains and forests. This is the middle to southern part of Africa. Giraffes are herbivores. That means they eat only plants. They eat leaves off the tops of trees, because their necks are so long. They often eat the leaves of acacia trees. Giraffes also spend 80 percent of their day eating. They can last longer than camels without water, sometimes surviving for weeks at a time without it. However, when giraffes do drink, they swallow up to 12 gallons (45 liters) at once.

Giraffes are so tall that predators cannot attack them easily. As a result, smaller giraffes tend to get attacked more often. Giraffes must be especially careful when they stop to drink. Predators try to attack giraffes often when their heads are bent down to water. But the giraffe is good at protecting itself. If needed, a giraffe can kick with enough force to kill a lion. However, giraffes often escape an attack and run away instead of fighting. Their legs are so long that they can run extremely fast and far in a very short time. Often, the closest we can get to these amazing animals is to see them in zoos.

Draw a line to match each word from the passage to its meaning. Then answer the questions below.

1. majority   a. animal that eats only plants

2. savanna   b. very, or particularly

3. herbivore   c. animal that hunts another animal

4. predator   d. the greatest number

5. especially   e. grassy plain with few trees

6. Which sentence from the passage tells how tall giraffes are when they are born?

_____

7. According to the passage, how are giraffes different from camels?

_____

8. How do adult giraffes often react when attacked by predators?

_____

First Lady of the Boston Marathon

What happens when a woman enters the 1967 Boston Marathon without anyone knowing that she's a woman? History is made!

Until the early 1970s, the Boston Marathon was an all-male tradition. One of the most world-famous running races was a "no girls allowed" event. That made female runners like twenty-year-old Kathrine Switzer feel left out. She wasn't the only one who felt that way, either. A year earlier, in 1966, a woman had run the marathon as an unofficial runner. She hid in bushes and then ran the race without being given an official number. But in 1967, Kathrine went one step further.

Kathrine signed up for the race under the name K.V. Switzer. Her plan worked. She was given a number, and she showed up for the race. She became the first woman to officially run in the Boston Marathon.

But not everyone was as pleased as Kathrine was. About four miles (six km) into the 26-mile (42-km) race, officials began trying to stop Kathrine. One of them even ran into the race and tried to push her out of the way. Other runners came to her rescue. She continued running. But she had gotten the attention of news reporters. While she ran, they asked her questions. They asked her why she was doing this. They wanted to know when she planned on quitting. They could not believe that a woman could actually finish a marathon like a man could. But Kathrine did finish the race.

Kathrine had inspired many other women. By 1972, women were officially allowed to run in the Boston Marathon. Today, thousands of women run in marathons all around the world. Kathrine still runs marathons and other running races. In 2011, she was inducted into the National Women's Hall of Fame. She still speaks for rights of women, especially in the world of sports.

_____ Women were officially allowed to run the Boston Marathon.

_____ Race officials tried to push Kathrine out of the race.

_____ The first woman ran the Boston Marathon unofficially.

_____ Marathon runners protected Kathrine and let her finish the race.

_____ Kathrine Switzer signed up for the Boston Marathon as K.V. Switzer.

_____ Kathrine ran the Boston Marathon in 1967.

Why were Kathrine Switzer's actions during the 1967 Boston Marathon considered brave?

_____

_____

Which sentence from the passage shows that Kathrine's story would not likely happen today?

_____

_____

Sharks

Sharks live in every ocean in the world. And these fish are always on the move. Sharks will migrate to find food, sometimes moving hundreds of miles at a time. These large changes in location mean the animal adapts, or adjusts, well to changes in its environment. Sharks are able to live in either cold or warm waters.

Sharks have an incredible sense of smell. Some sharks, like the lemon shark, can sense if there is a single drop of blood in 25 gallons (95 liters) of water! And some sharks can even smell blood a quarter mile (0.4 km) away. Many humans are afraid of sharks because they are such skilled hunters. They are normally thought of as being some of the most dangerous animals in the ocean. But the number of deaths due to shark attacks is actually very low. Only about five humans die per year from a shark attack. Scientists think the reason for this is that sharks spend their time in deep waters. They also prefer to eat other ocean animals.

Scientists have discovered more than four hundred different species of sharks, and there may be many more. Some of the most popular sharks are the Great White and the Hammerhead. Both of these animals got their names based on how they look. The Great White shark grows to be about 3,000 pounds (1.4 metric tons) and 12 feet (3.6 m) long! The Hammerhead has a long, flat head, similar to the shape of a hammer. Tiger sharks are known for eating anything that they find. They have been found with alarm clocks and boat parts in their stomachs! Hopefully we will find out a lot more about these amazing creatures in the future.

Circle the true statements.

1. Sharks are found only in warm ocean waters.

2. Sharks have an excellent sense of smell.

3. Sharks mainly attack humans when they are looking for food.

4. Sharks do not have to move very far when looking for food.

5. There are more than four hundred species of sharks.

6. The Hammerhead shark is the largest shark species in the world.

7. Great White sharks can grow to be 12 feet (3.6 m) long.

8. Scientists are not sure what Tiger sharks eat.

Gold Rush!

Imagine looking into a river and seeing gold glitter and sparkle in the water. That's what happened in 1848 when James W. Marshall looked into a river at Sutter's Mill, a sawmill in Coloma, California. Word spread fast that the mineral was in high supply around the area.

The Gold Rush began quickly. People learned how to "pan" for gold. They scooped up water and silt from riverbeds in wide, shallow pans. Then they swirled the water until the silt settled and they could see the gold in the bottom of the pan. They sold the gold for high prices. Some people got rich quickly. Some worked hard but never found much gold.

About 300,000 people left their lives to move to California in hopes of getting rich. These people became known as forty-niners, because they made their move in 1849. People arrived in California from all around the world. Some even came from as far away as Australia. Many of these travelers arrived on ships that anchored in San Francisco Bay. Some stayed in San Francisco. The city grew so quickly, it became known as a "boomtown."

The total amount of gold found during the Gold Rush was worth close to tens of billions of today's dollars. However, some merchants made even more money than the forty-niners. The boomtowns needed stores. Thousands of people had to buy food and set up homes. Businesspeople made money by selling goods to miners.

By 1855, the Gold Rush began to wind down. Most of the gold had all been mined and sold. The forty-niners had taken most of the gold from an entire state, with some getting rich, and some not. Once it was all done, boomtowns were abandoned. San Francisco remained an important city in California. But some of the other boomtowns became known as ghost towns.

Draw a line to match each word from the passage to its meaning. Then answer the questions below.

1. mineral

2. pan

3. boomtown

4. merchant

5. forty-niner

a. to swirl water and silt in a wide, shallow pan

b. a person who owns or runs a business

c. a natural substance found in the ground, such as gold

d. a person who went to California in 1849 to find gold

e. a town that goes through very fast growth

6. Summarize the passage.

_____

_____

_____

7. What process was used to get gold from rivers during the Gold Rush?

_____

_____

_____

8. Why did the California Gold Rush end?

_____

_____

Benefits of Biking

There's a saying that states that once you learn to ride a bike you never forget how to do it. Well, that's a good thing, because biking can provide a lifetime of great health benefits.

Cycling is great exercise in many ways. First of all, it's a wonderful way to get outdoors and breathe in some fresh air. Biking also helps build muscles in many parts of the body. The legs get a tough workout when you bike. But you can control how hard you cycle. You can bike faster or slower to control how hard you work. Many bikes have settings that can make it easier to pedal, if needed. That way, there's no excuse for being too tired! You can just change the bike to a speed that makes it easier to pedal.

Biking can help control your weight. It keeps your heart healthy, too. That's because your muscles stay in motion. Biking has even been found to help prevent certain diseases. That's because the body stays active and healthy when you bike!

A bike rider is likely to have better balance and coordination than someone who does not ride a bike. Just think about what you are doing as you bike. You are staying balanced on two wheels. At the same time, your legs pump up and down. You are steering the bike as well. The brain is constantly sending messages to your muscles. This helps keep you from falling over. Your mind stays active as you keep an eye out for traffic.

In addition to having health benefits, biking also helps you get around! Biking to school, the store, and just about anywhere else can help save on gasoline. Next time you need a ride, rely on your muscle power instead!

Use the words to complete the sentences below.

disease   outdoors   coordination   brain

gasoline   heart   speed   pedaling

1. Biking is a great exercise for your _____.

2. It takes _____ to stay balanced on two wheels.

3. While biking, your _____ is sending messages to and from your muscles.

4. If you are tired when biking, you can change the _____ setting on the bike.

5. Another way to control your biking is to speed up or slow down your _____.

6. Staying active with biking can help to prevent _____.

7. Biking _____ is a great way to get fresh air.

8. Biking helps the environment because it doesn't use _____.

Animals in the White House

US presidents are no strangers to pets. Presidents have owned some pretty strange animals, too. Thomas Jefferson's pets included two bear cubs, while John Quincy Adams had silkworms as pets. Martin Van Buren even owned two tiger cubs for a short amount of time. James Buchanan kept an elephant at the White House. Benjamin Harrison had two opossums, and Theodore Roosevelt had a small zoo at the White House. Just a few of his many animals included a snake, a rat, a pig, a hyena, an owl, and even a one-legged rooster. But the most popular pet in the presidential palace has always been the dog.

The chart shows that there has been a presidential pooch in the White House every single term since 1901. The chart shows that dogs aren't just man's best friend. They are also a president's best friend.

Number	President	Years	Number of Dogs in White House
26	Theodore Roosevelt	1901–1909	10
27	William Howard Taft	1909–1913	1
28	Woodrow Wilson	1913–1921	3
29	Warren G. Harding	1921–1923	3
30	Calvin Coolidge	1923–1929	12
31	Herbert Hoover	1929–1933	9
32	Franklin D. Roosevelt	1933–1945	7
33	Harry S. Truman	1945–1953	2
34	Dwight D. Eisenhower	1953–1961	1
35	John F. Kennedy	1961–1963	8
36	Lyndon B. Johnson	1963–1969	6
37	Richard M. Nixon	1969–1974	3
38	Gerald Ford	1974–1977	2
39	Jimmy Carter	1977–1981	2
40	Ronald Reagan	1981–1989	6
41	George H.W. Bush	1989–1993	2
42	Bill Clinton	1993–2001	1
43	George W. Bush	2001–2009	3
44	Barack Obama	2009–2016	2

Read each question and circle the correct answer.

1. Which pets did Thomas Jefferson have in the White House?

   a) snake   **b)** elephant   **c)** tiger cubs   **d)** bear cubs

2. Which president had a one-legged rooster in the White House?

   a) Theodore Roosevelt   **b)** James Buchanan

   c) Martin Van Buren   **d)** John Quincy Adams

3. Which has been the most popular animal for presidents to keep in the White House?

   a) cat   **b)** dog   **c)** bird   **d)** fish

4. How many dogs did Richard Nixon have in the White House?

   a) 1   **b)** 2   **c)** 3   **d)** 4

5. Which president had the most dogs in the White House?

   a) Theodore Roosevelt   **b)** Calvin Coolidge

   c) Herbert Hoover   **d)** Lyndon B. Johnson

6. How many dogs lived in the White House in the years 1933–1945?

   a) 1   **b)** 3   **c)** 7   **d)** 10

7. How many dogs lived in the White House during Woodrow Wilson and Warren G. Harding's presidencies?

   a) 2   **b)** 4   **c)** 6   **d)** 8

8. Which president had only one dog living in the White House?

   a) Harry S. Truman   **b)** Bill Clinton

   c) John F. Kennedy   **d)** Barack Obama

Earthquake Shake

An earthquake is a sudden shaking of the ground. Several million earthquakes happen every year! That's about fifty earthquakes somewhere in the world each day. Don't worry, though. Many of the earthquakes that happen around the world are not even felt by humans.

So what causes these quakes? The surface of Earth is made up of sections called plates. These plates move and bump up against each other. We only feel the strongest of these quakes. But scientists still try to keep track of all of them. They use a scale that measures the movements of the plates. The scale is called a Richter scale. It was named after the scientist who invented it.

The chart shows the possible scores on the Richter scale. Next to that, it shows the type of effects that people would feel from that kind of earthquake. You will see that some cannot be felt. Others cause total destruction of property. Out of the several million earthquakes per year, only about one earthquake scores 8 or higher on the Richter scale. Only fifteen have a reading of about 7. So, it's true that Earth is always rocking and shaking. But humans usually have a very steady ride.

Richter Scale Reading	Effect on Humans
less than 1–2.9	Not usually felt by humans
3–3.9	Ceiling lights sway
4–4.9	Walls may crack
5–5.9	Furniture moves
6–6.9	Some buildings fall
7–7.9	Many buildings are destroyed
8 and up	Severe destruction of buildings, roads, bridges

1. How many earthquakes happen every year?

    a) several   **b)** several hundred   **c)** several thousand   **d)** several million

2. What is the purpose of the Richter scale?

    a) to measure the timing of earthquakes

    b) to measure the movement of Earth's plates

    c) to count the number of earthquakes that happen each day

    d) to count the number of earthquakes that happen each year

3. What causes earthquakes?

    a) movement of Earth's plates   **b)** high winds

    c) strong ocean waves   **d)** changes in Earth's weather

4. About how many earthquakes per year are felt by humans?

    a) all   **b)** most   **c)** some   **d)** none

5. About how many earthquakes per year score 8 or above on the Richter scale?

    a) 1   **b)** 15   **c)** 50   **d)** 1,000

6. What reading on the Richter scale may cause walls in homes to crack?

    a) 2–2.9   **b)** 3–3.9   **c)** 4–4.9   **d)** 5–5.9

7. What might happen to property during an earthquake that has a 3 reading on the Richter scale?

    a) Furniture may move.   **b)** Buildings may fall.

    c) Ceilings lights may sway.   **d)** Humans do not feel it.

8. Which of the following readings on a Richter scale shows a minor earthquake?

    a) 2–3   **b)** 4–5   **c)** 6–7   **d)** 8

Steve Jobs

Are you a creative person who understands electronics? Then you could have a chance of becoming the next Steve Jobs. Born in 1955, Steve Jobs grew up in California. As a child, Jobs worked with his father on electronics. They used the family garage to take them apart and put them back together. This taught Jobs a lot about mechanics.

In high school, Jobs met Steve Wozniak. By 1976, the two started a business together, called Apple Computer. Working again out of the Jobses' garage and home, the business took off. For the very first time, they introduced a personal computer to the world. The computer was cheap enough and small enough for people to buy. It was also the first time an average person could operate a computer because it was so easy to use.

The Apple computer was such an important invention that it still affects the way everyone today lives. The computer paved the way for the entire personal computer market. Now, most households have at least one personal computer. We rely on personal computers at home, work, and school. We also rely on other Apple products such as the iPod, iPhone, and iPad.

Steve Jobs designed how many Apple products looked. He wanted everything to look neat and clean. He even tried to make the inside of the products look nice. When Apple made the iMac, it said, "the back of our computer looks better than the front of anyone else's." Even after Steve Jobs's death in 2011, his company continues to play an important part in how we see the future of technology.

Read each statement. Write *true* or *false*. Then answer the question below.

1. Steve Jobs grew up in California. _____

2. Steve Jobs started Apple Computer with Steve Wozniak. _____

3. The first Apple computer was too difficult for most people to understand how to use. _____

4. The company started inside the Jobs family's garage and home. _____

5. It took a long time for the personal computer to catch on with the public. _____

6. Steve Jobs was not concerned with the way the products he invented looked. _____

7. Today most households have at least one personal computer. _____

8. Bonus: What did Steve Jobs do as a child that helped him to become an inventor as an adult?

_____

_____

Yellowstone National Park

If you've ever visited national parks in the United States, you'd know that they offer amazing chances to see the beauty of nature. Yellowstone National Park is located in the states of Wyoming, Idaho, and Montana. In 1872, it was the first area in the United States to be preserved, or saved, as a national park. Since then, many other areas have been set aside as national parks.

There's a lot to admire at Yellowstone. There are about three hundred bird species and many other animals to observe. The area has lakes, rivers, mountains, and canyons. But it is the area underneath the park that makes Yellowstone so unique.

The ground below Yellowstone is part of a very large supervolcano that creates beautiful land features in the area. For example, there are three hundred geysers in the park. A geyser is a hot, underground spring. It shoots a tall stream of water and steam high into the air. In addition to these geysers and hot springs, the park also has areas of boiling, bubbling mud!

One of the park's most famous geysers, called Old Faithful, erupts about once every 90 minutes. Another geyser in the park, called Steamboat Geyser, is the world's tallest geyser. It shoots water more than 300 feet (91 m) into the air.

In 1883, railroads were built to help people reach Yellowstone more easily. In 1915, cars were allowed into the park for the first time. Today people visit the park from all around the world. Each person experiences something a little different about the landscape. Some visit to see Old Faithful erupt. Others visit to hike, swim, and just enjoy the beautiful scenery.

1. When was Yellowstone made into a national park?

_____

2. What underground feature at Yellowstone makes the area unique?

_____

3. What is a geyser?

_____

4. How can you describe Old Faithful and Steamboat Springs geysers at Yellowstone?

_____

5. Why are the geysers and mud pools at Yellowstone hot?

_____

6. How did Yellowstone Park change in 1883?

_____

7. How did the park change in 1915?

_____

8. What are some activities that visitors to Yellowstone can do?

_____

_____

Bat Talk

You might see one at sunset, flying across the darkened sky. You can tell it is not a bird. It doesn't fly straight like a bird. It dives and swoops. Its wings flap oddly. What is this creature in the sky? It's a bat!

Even though bats have wings and fly, they're actually mammals! They are the only mammals that can fly.

Many bats live in caves. They often live and sleep in family groups. They might live in groups of hundreds, hanging upside down to rest and sleep. Bats eat insects and will sometimes eat small animals. They also eat nectar from plants. Bats often swoop through the air, catching mosquitoes in their mouths as they fly.

Bats have a special way of finding their food. Instead of using their sense of smell or sight, like other animals, bats use their sense of sound. Echolocation is a kind of communication that uses high-frequency sounds. The bat sends out signals that bounce off objects around it. The signal then bounces back to the bat. This lets the bat know exactly where an object is located around it. The bat can instantly figure out the size, shape, and texture of the object.

Bats live in most regions around the world, except for large deserts or polar regions. Some live very close to people, too. They may show up in backyards or even in the attics of homes. While some species of bats are doing very well, others are endangered. The Gray Bat, the Ozark Big-Eared Bat, and the Indiana Bat are all nearing extinction. The good news is that some of these bats are making a comeback. There was a 40 percent increase in some of these populations between 1993 and 2011. That's good news for this unique flying mammal.

Circle the best word or phrase to complete each sentence.

1. Bats are the only known flying _____.

   reptile   mammal

2. When bats fly, they look most similar to _____.

   birds   insects

3. Bats are often found living in _____ in family groups.

   bushes   caves

4. Echolocation is a form of communication that uses _____.

   sound   smell

5. Bats use echolocation to find _____ to eat.

   large mammals   small insects

6. Bats are NOT found in _____ areas.

   forested   polar

7. The Ozark Big-Eared Bat is _____.

   endangered   extinct

8. Since the 1990s, some populations of endangered bats have
   _____.

   increased   decreased

Unicorns of the Sea

Have you ever seen a narwhal? If you have, you might think it looks funny. It looks like a whale with a giant sword sticking out of its head! The narwhal is actually one of the rarest whales in the sea. The long, sword-like tusk grows on the head of male narwhals. It gives them the nickname

"unicorns of the sea." Male narwhals have been seen touching tusks with each other. This may be a form of dueling. It may be a way to communicate.

The tusk on the head of the narwhal is actually a long tooth. It grows from the upper jaw of the animal. It can be used to spear prey. Narwhals eat shrimp, squid, and many types of fish.

Narwhals travel in groups called pods. It is typical to see a pod of ten to a hundred narwhals in Arctic regions between Russia and Greenland. Because they are mammals, narwhals often stay near the ocean surface. This allows them to easily come up for air to breathe.

Narwhals normally move slowly in the water. But they can pick up speed very quickly. They swim fast if they are trying to escape a predator. Polar bears and orca whales are their greatest predators.

Changes to the Arctic climate have made the narwhal's home a more difficult place to live. The waters are warmer. This means there is a smaller food supply. It has to swim farther from its natural habitat to find food. People are stepping up to help the narwhal, however. If we can preserve natural habitats, the narwhal will continue to amaze people as the unicorn of the sea.

Answer the questions.

1. Paraphrase what the passage says about the narwhal's long tusk.

   _____

   _____

2. Why do you think the narwhal's nickname is "unicorn of the sea"?

   _____

3. Which sentence from the passage describes the narwhal's prey?

   _____

4. Why wouldn't a narwhal be spotted in warm waters in tropical oceans?

   _____

5. What countries does the passage mention that narwhals travel between?

   _____

6. How do narwhals travel in the ocean?

   _____

7. According to the passage, why do narwhals stay near the surface of the ocean?

   _____

   _____

8. What are two reasons that narwhals are in danger?

   _____

   _____

Landfills

How much trash do people put into landfills each year? Too much! Did you know that on average, each American generates about 4.6 pounds (2 kg) of trash each and every day? That's almost double the amount of trash per person of most other nations. According to the Environmental Protection Agency, that adds up to 251 million tons (227 million metric tons) each year in the United States.

What happens to all of this trash? About 32 percent is recycled. About 12 percent is burned. About 55 percent is buried in landfills. Landfills continue to grow, as more are built over the surface of our precious land.

The news about landfills is not all bad. The trash is not simply dumped onto the ground and piled as high as a mountain. Landfills are designed to keep from polluting the surrounding area. Liners come between the trash and the soil. This helps to keep the trash from polluting the soil. It is kept away from water sources or other areas that can easily become contaminated. It is covered in soil so that rain cannot wash it away. Special systems are put in place to drain water away safely so that it does not come in contact with the environment.

So why should we be concerned with the number of landfills? The problem is that we are simply running out of room! The more landfills, the less natural our land becomes. Mistakes at landfills can cause dangerous pollution. Plants and animals have less room to live and grow. Let's look for a different solution than covering our land with trash!

Read each statement. Write *fact* or *opinion*. Then answer the question below.

1. Too much trash is placed in landfills. _____

2. Each American makes about 4.6 pounds
   (2 kg) of trash each day. _____

3. About 32 percent of trash is recycled. _____

4. Landfills are built on liners to protect soil. _____

5. Too much of our land is covered in trash. _____

6. Landfills give plants and animals less
   room to live and grow. _____

7. We need different solutions to landfills. _____

8. Now write your opinion about landfills.

_____

_____

_____

_____

Juliette Gordon Low

What are the traits you think of when you think of a Girl Scout? You might think of a strong, independent, hard-working leader. Those are the same traits of the founder of the Girl Scouts. Her name is Juliette Gordon Low.

Born in 1860 in Savannah, Georgia, Juliette's family nicknamed her "Daisy." They made sure she got a good education. In addition to going to school, Daisy was taught skills such as painting and sculpture. She learned to swim, canoe, and play tennis. She liked to sketch, write poems, and act in plays. It's no wonder that these are some of the many activities that today's Girl Scouts take part in.

In 1911, Juliette discovered something she could do to help girls everywhere. She wanted them to have the same opportunities that she had. She met the founder of the Boy Scouts, Robert Baden-Powell. Juliette started a similar group for girls. She called it the Girl Guides. Soon after, the name was changed to Girl Scouts.

The group did something no group had done before. It gave girls from all different backgrounds the chance to learn and grow. It taught skills that made girls rely on themselves instead of others. At the time, this was unusual. Girls learned skills for business, home life, and the outdoors. They learned to become leaders. The Girl Scouts was one of the first groups to welcome members with disabilities. Juliette thought this was important. She was deaf in one ear. She was eventually deaf in both ears. She understood some of the challenges that disabled people faced.

What's the proof that the Girl Scouts is a success? The Girl Guides started with just eighteen members. Today, there are 2.8 million members of the Girl Scouts in America!

Read each question and circle the correct answer. Then answer the questions below.

1. What nickname did Juliette Gordon Low's family give her?

   a) Julie   b) Jules   c) Daisy   d) Flower

2. Which activity does the passage NOT mention as a skill that Juliette learned as a child?

   a) swimming   b) canoeing   c) singing   d) painting

3. Which event in Juliette's life inspired her to start the Girl Scouts?

   a) getting an education   b) learning to paint and sculpt

   c) opening a hospital for soldiers   d) meeting the founder of the Boy Scouts

4. What kind of member did Juliette think was important to allow into the Girl Scouts?

   a) disabled   b) educated   c) boys   d) adults

5. Why did Juliette think it was important for girls to learn to rely on themselves?

   a) Parents requested it.   b) She grew up relying on others.

   c) Girls were not allowed in school.   d) Many girls relied on others.

6. How many members were in the first group of Girl Guides?

   a) 3   b) 18   c) 200   d) 2.8 million

7. How did Juliette's childhood influence activities that the Girl Scouts do?

   _____

   _____

8. What kind of disability did Juliette have, and how did it affect her life?

   _____

   _____

How to Run for Class President

Some elementary schools have a group called student government. It is made up of students who help to make rules for the whole school. The student government might also help to ask the school for things that students need or want. They work with adults in the school to get these things done.

Just as with a real government, a student government often has a president. Students take a vote to decide which candidate would do the best job.

If you are interested in becoming a class president, here are a few tips:

Make sure you want the job! Being class president can be a tough job. It might mean going to many meetings and working with students and teachers. If you are dedicated, others will notice!

Work with a friend to make and hang posters around the school. Make sure your posters are interesting and eye-catching. They should show your full name and at least one reason students should vote for you.

Be responsible. Students want to vote for the person they think will do the best job. So being a good student is one way to show your classmates that you will be able to get the job done.

Decide what you stand for. Let people know what you plan to do as president. This will help them decide if they want to vote for you.

Be nice to classmates! As the student president, you will have to work with many people. Students and teachers should feel that you are a good person to work with. Show that you can be pleasant and friendly. It will pay off!

Circle the best word or phrase to complete each sentence.

1. One job of the student government is to make _____ for the class or school.

   rules   jobs

2. People decide who will be president by _____.

   trying each person   voting for one person

3. Before running for class president, be sure you want the job because

   _____.

   it can be difficult   you will have to quit school to do it

4. A friend can help you _____ if you want to run for president.

   make up new rules   hang posters

5. Your posters should be _____ and eye-catching.

   funny   interesting

6. A person who wants to be class president and gets good grades shows that he or she is _____.

   responsible   only interested in grades

7. According to the passage, people will know if they want to vote for you as class president if you _____.

   make a two-minute speech   make your ideas known

8. A person who can be friendly will make a good president because he or she will have to _____.

   work well with others   get things done quickly

Camping without a Trace

You are excited about a camping trip. You can't wait to get out into the woods. You love the great outdoors, but how will you show your respect for the environment? Did you know that the best campers are the ones who leave nature just as they found it? On your next camping trip, try to camp without leaving a trace!

Plan ahead so you are able to deal with all of the trash you make. Food packages and anything else you bring into the woods must also be removed when you leave.

Use campsites that have already been cleared. There is no reason to clear more areas of a wooded site. Leave rocks, trees, and other plants the way you found them. Don't build ditches or other holes in the ground that can change the way water flows.

Be careful about any firewood you bring into the area. It may introduce new insects. It can introduce new seeds into the area as well. This can end up changing the environment. Instead, use wood that has already fallen. Or buy firewood sold by the campground.

Observe the wildlife from a distance. Don't feed any animals you find in the wild. This can make them sick. It can also make them depend on people for food in the future.

Never leave a campfire until you know it is completely out. Millions of acres of forests a year are destroyed by forest fires set by people. These fires move about 14 miles (22 km) per hour. They can destroy everything in their path.

When you are in nature, be considerate of other campers. Enjoy the quiet beauty of nature, and let other campers do the same!

Answer the questions.

1. Write a summary of the first paragraph.

_____

_____

2. How can campers bring food on their trip without adding pollution to the area?

_____

_____

3. While choosing a campsite, what is one way to leave a wooded area the same way you found it?

_____

_____

4. According to the passage, how can bringing your own firewood to a campsite damage the environment?

_____

5. What tip does the passage give about helping preserve the wildlife in an area?

_____

6. Summarize the information the passage gives about forest fires.

_____

_____

7. Why should you be considerate of other people when you are camping?

_____

8. Summarize the whole passage in one sentence.

_____

Animal Night Life

When nighttime falls in a forest, more than just the stars come out. There are a bunch of nocturnal animals that keep the woods alive all night long. Here are just a few examples:

Owls

Owls have great eyesight and hearing that allows them to spot their prey in the dark. Just think about how large their eyes and ears are in comparison to their head. They can also twist their heads more than halfway around. This lets them see what is happening all around them. Their stiff feathers help them fly without being heard. Watch out, snakes and mice!

Raccoons

Raccoons look like masked bandits of the night. They sleep during the day and get up at night to hunt for food. Like the owl, raccoons have great vision for finding their way in the darkness. They eat fruits, nuts, berries, and plants. They even eat small animals such as frogs and rodents.

Skunks

It's hard to miss the smell of a skunk! This nocturnal animal keeps predators away by spraying them with an oily liquid from under its long, fluffy tail. The strong smell can stay in the air for days. The animal's bold, black-and-white striped fur may help other animals recognize it so they keep their distance. These handy features allow skunks to look for food without much trouble.

Opossums

The only pouched animal in North America only comes out at night. The female opossum has a pouch on its belly for its babies. When the babies grow a bit older, they ride on their mom's back. How does this animal stay safe from predators? It plays dead! It will lie still, stick out its tongue, and hope the predator moves right along.

By the time morning comes, each of these nocturnal animals needs some shut-eye.

Write two facts about each nocturnal animal discussed in the passage.

1. Owl

_____

_____

2. Raccoon

_____

_____

3. Skunk

_____

_____

4. Opossum

_____

_____

Pizza Rolls

Follow this recipe for a delicious and simple snack that tastes like pizza! Ask an adult for help to bake this tasty treat.

Ingredients

package of prepared biscuit
  or crescent roll dough
mozzarella cheese
pepperoni slices
olive oil
Parmesan cheese, grated
marinara sauce, warmed

Method

1. Flatten the dough on a table. Cut the dough into squares about 4 inches by 4 inches (10 cm by 10 cm).

2. Place a slice of mozzarella cheese on each square.

3. Lay slices of pepperoni on top of the center of the cheese. Roll up the dough square and press on the seam to keep it closed.

4. Place each roll on a greased baking sheet with the seam facing down.

5. Brush olive oil over each pizza roll, then sprinkle with Parmesan cheese.

6. Bake in a 425 degrees Farenheit (218 degrees C) oven for about 20 minutes. The dough should be golden brown and the cheese inside should be melted.

7. Ask an adult for help removing the rolls from the oven. Let them cool for five minutes before tasting them.

8. Warm the marinara sauce on the stovetop or in the microwave oven. Dip each roll in sauce and enjoy!

What's the order? Write 1, 2, 3, 4, 5, 6, 7 on the lines. Then answer the question below.

_____ Roll up the dough squares to enclose the mozzarella and pepperoni.

_____ Cut the dough into squares.

_____ Bake pizza rolls at 425° F (218° C) for 20 minutes.

_____ Roll the dough out on a table.

_____ Brush olive oil and sprinkle Parmesan cheese on the rolls on baking sheet.

_____ Place mozzarella cheese and pepperoni on top of dough squares.

_____ When the pizza rolls cool, dunk them in warmed marinara sauce and enjoy.

What other items besides the food ingredients does someone need to follow the recipe?

_____

_____

_____

Write a Great Thank-You Note

When someone does something nice for you, how do you respond? If you are with the person at the time, it's okay to just say thanks in person. But other times, a thank-you note is best.

A thank-you note is a great way to express just how much you appreciate something. It shows that you understand that someone went out of his or her way to help you. Even if it is for something as simple as a small present, it helps to write a heartfelt note.

First, clearly state what you are thanking the person for. Is it for coming to a party, giving you a gift, or both? Did the person also do anything else special on that day, such as bringing food, chairs, decorations, or flowers to your party? Mention each thing. Tell the person how much it all meant to you. Use words such as *thoughtful, generous*, and *kind* to describe the things the person did for you.

Finally, tell how much his or her actions meant to you. That might mean thanking the person for spending an important time in your life with you. It might mean thanking the person for surprising you. Tell the person how it made you feel. You can also offer to return the favor so that person will know you can be counted on.

Don't wait too long to send your thank-you note. Sending it promptly is one good step toward being a good friend.

1. Thank-you notes should always be sent whenever someone does something for you. _____

2. Each thing a person does for you at a birthday celebration should receive a separate thank-you note. _____

3. Thank-you notes are usually given only to thank people for gifts. _____

4. Words such as *thoughtful* and *generous* are useful words for thank-you notes. _____

5. Thank-you notes should be sent promptly. _____

6. According to the passage, what are some reasons a person should send a thank-you note?

_____

_____

7. Why is it important to thank someone for something he or she did for you?

_____

_____

8. Why might someone offer his or her help in a thank-you note to the person receiving the note?

_____

_____

Technologies of Tomorrow

When you think of the future of technology, do you think of flying cars and robots? Whatever you may think, there is no doubt that technology is always advancing. Futurists are people who make predictions about the future based on what is happening now. Many futurists think that we may not be far off from sending people to Mars or sending average citizens deep into space.

But what is happening closer to home? How is technology changing the way we live? There's some good news and some bad news in our technologies of tomorrow. The bad news is there are many hackers stealing people's personal information, or identities. This is becoming a problem. People do a lot of private business on the Internet. That means that their personal information can be stolen. New technologies must try to deal with this problem and make our information safer online.

The good news about technology is that there are infinite, or an endless number of, possibilities of what we can do. For example, virtual reality is a technology in which a person puts on a headset and feels part of a different world. The technology tricks the mind into thinking that it is in the world that it sees in the headset. Video games first developed the technology. However, it is now expanding to new areas. For example, a soldier in training can wear a virtual reality headset. The soldier can then react as if he or she is in the scene. The imaginary scene can provide new experiences. The soldier can train safely.

Technologies like virtual reality can change our perception, or understanding, of the world. Technology can change the way we think. That means it can change the way we live and learn.

Draw a line to match each word from the passage to its meaning. Then answer the questions below.

1. futurist

    a. person who uses computers to get private information

2. virtual reality

    b. a technology that uses a headset to show the viewer a different scene

3. hacker

    c. an endless number

4. infinite

    d. a person's understanding of the world

5. perception

    e. a person who predicts what the future will be like

6. Now summarize the passage.

_____

_____

_____

7. What is one way that technology needs to improve in the future?

_____

_____

8. How can a soldier train with virtual reality technology?

_____

_____

Get Your Fruits and Veggies!

THE DAILY NEWS

Letters to the Editor

Dear Editor:

Children today don't get enough fruits and vegetables. We can't blame these children, either. It's their parents who don't give them the food they need to be healthy and grow strong.

I think parents could do a better job at giving children what they need. I think children could be stronger and smarter as a result. Giving kids more fruits and vegetables is a good way to start them out eating right.

According to the American Heart Association, fruits and vegetables are very important. They have the vitamins, minerals, and fiber that people need for good health. An active ten-year-old boy needs 1.5 cups (360 ml) of fruits and 2.5 cups (590 ml) of vegetables each day. A cup of fruit is equal to one apple, banana, pear, orange, or grapefruit. A cup of fruit is also equal to eight strawberries or two plums. A cup of vegetables is one stalk of celery or a corncob. It's a potato or a dozen baby carrots.

Those foods should be easy enough for any child to get. Each one of those foods would make a great snack. But too many children don't eat these for snacks. I think many get away with eating junk food instead.

As a nurse, I see sick children all day long. It's part of my job. I know that children would be much healthier if they ate the right foods.

I'm writing this letter to all the parents out there who allow their kids to snack to their heart's content. I plead with you—give your kids more fruits and veggies! You'll be happier because you'll have healthier kids!

Sincerely,
Nurse Tina Almun

Read each statement. Write *fact* or *opinion*. Then answer the questions below.

1. Children today don't get enough fruits and vegetables. _____

2. Fruits and vegetables have vitamins, minerals, and fiber. _____

3. An active ten-year-old boy needs 1.5 cups (360 ml) of fruit each day. _____

4. One cup of fruit is equal to eight strawberries. _____

5. Parents let their kids eat too many unhealthy snacks. _____

6. Which words in the second paragraph show that the author is giving an opinion? _____

7. Which paragraph from the passage lists all facts?

_____

8. Write your own opinion about healthy eating.

_____

_____

Green Monster Smoothie

Green smoothies are a great way to get the fruits and vegetables you need to stay healthy and strong. Just one smoothie has all of the fruits and most of the vegetables you will need for the day. It can sometimes be hard to eat a lot of vegetables at once. But a smoothie is a fast and delicious way to do it.

Smoothies don't always have to be green, either. You can change some of the ingredients in the smoothie to other fruits. Strawberries and bananas usually work well. Just remember to include water or some other kind of liquid. That will help the foods combine easily.

The Green Monster Smoothie includes as much cucumber and spinach as you might eat during a meal. When it's mixed with fruits, it tastes sweeter. Maybe you're someone who doesn't care for spinach. That's all right. You will probably find that you can't even taste it in the smoothie. Have an adult help you put all of these ingredients into a blender and enjoy!

Ingredients

1 cup ice cubes
1 cup fresh spinach
1 kiwi, peeled and sliced
1 green apple, peeled and sliced
1 green pear, peeled and sliced
1 cucumber, peeled and sliced
1 cup water

Method

Place all of the ingredients into a blender. Mix it on the highest setting for one minute. If you have extra, share some with a friend!

1. Which of the following is NOT an ingredient in the Green Monster Smoothie?

   a) spinach   **b)** kiwi   **c)** oatmeal   **d)** apple

2. Why does the author suggest that the reader get an adult to help?

   a) The ingredients are difficult to find.   **b)** A high-speed blender can be dangerous.

   c) The ingredients have to be washed.   **d)** Some of the ingredients are dangerous.

3. How long does the recipe suggest that the smoothie be blended?

   a) 3–5 seconds   **b)** 3–5 minutes   **c)** 1 second   **d)** 1 minute

4. Why is the smoothie called a Green Monster?

   a) All of the ingredients are green.   **b)** The ingredients are overripe.

   c) It tastes "monstrously" bad.   **d)** The smoothie's name has no meaning.

5. How does the author suggest that someone can change the recipe?

   a) Add water.   **b)** Replace the fruits.

   c) Remove the fruits.   **d)** Remove the vegetables.

6. Why might someone not be able to taste the spinach in the smoothie?

   a) The spinach is combined with so many fruits.

   b) The recipe calls for less than a half cup of spinach.

   c) The recipe calls for ten other foods in addition to spinach.

   d) The spinach is removed from the smoothie before drinking.

7. How does the author compare the smoothie to the foods you might eat during a meal?

   _____

8. How does the author describe the taste of the smoothie?

   _____

Snakes

If you cross paths with a snake, you might be alarmed. This slithery reptile has been known to scare off more than just its enemies in the animal world. Humans fear snakes more than they do most other animals.

Many snakes are harmless to humans. For example, there's no reason to fear the garter snake. Many are 2 to 3 feet (0.6 to 0.9 m) long and found in forests all over North America. Some people even keep these harmless animals as pets. All snakes are carnivores, which means that they eat other animals. The garter snake eats small animals such as mice.

Other snakes live up to their frightening reputation. The king cobra is one of the most dangerous snakes in the world. It is found mostly in Asia and usually avoids humans. However, a single bite from a king cobra contains enough venom, or poison, to kill up to twenty humans. It is also so long that it could lift up only a third of itself, and still be able to look a 6-foot-tall (1.8-m) person in the eyes!

Many snakes kill their prey with venom. Others squeeze their prey by constricting it. That means they wrap themselves around their prey. They squeeze so tightly they kill the animal. Snakes can also eat things much larger than themselves by unhinging their jaw. This helps them eat their prey whole, without even chewing! After the snake digests the animal, it spits out the bones.

There are almost 3,000 different species of snakes in the world. Only a very small number of these are harmful to humans. The problem is, it's hard to tell which ones they are! The solution? The more you learn about snakes, the safer you will be!

1. carnivore

    a. belief or opinion held by many people about something

2. reputation

    b. removing hinges or movable joints

3. venom

    c. an animal that eats other animals

4. constricting

    d. holding tightly and squeezing

5. unhinging

    e. poisonous liquid made by the body of a snake or other animal

6. Summarize the passage.

_____

_____

_____

7. What are two ways that snakes can kill their prey?

_____

_____

8. How does a snake eat prey that is much larger than it?

_____

_____

Rules of Soccer

The rules of soccer are easy to understand. Two teams play against each other on a long, rectangular field. The field is divided in half, and each half has a goal. A goal is a pair of posts linked with a bar across the top. A goal usually has a net that encloses it in the back.

The object of the game is for each team to get the soccer ball into the opposing team's goal. The team with the most points wins the game.

The only person allowed to use his or her hands is the goalie, or person guarding the goal against kicked balls. Other members can use any other part of their body to control the ball. Most players kick the ball. But many also control it by using their knees, shoulders, chest, and even their head.

Teams start the game by facing each other in the center of the field. Each team faces the opposite goal and each other. Players try to kick the ball away from the other team. They then continue kicking and moving the ball toward the other team's goal line.

The number of players allowed on the field at once depends on the age of the players. There may be anywhere from eight to eleven players on each team.

A referee plays an important role in a soccer game. He or she makes sure that everyone plays by the rules. There are many types of behaviors that can make a referee state that a "foul" has been made. This can include using hands during play. It can also mean behavior such as hitting, tripping, or fighting. A foul often results in a free goal kick for the opposite team. The best way to play soccer is to play fair and have fun!

Read each statement. Write *true* or *false*. Then answer the questions below.

1. A goalie is a person who makes sure the rules are followed. _____

2. Each team can have as many players as they want. _____

3. Soccer players use their feet, knees, shoulders, chest, and head to control the ball. _____

4. Each soccer game starts with teams facing each other. _____

5. Hitting or tripping another player may result in a foul. _____

6. What is the purpose of a referee in a soccer game?

_____

7. What is the purpose of a goalie in a soccer game?

_____

_____

8. According to the passage, what is the best way to play soccer?

_____

_____

No Bones About It!

What's inside your body? Your bones make up your body's skeleton. The bones connect to help you move. Without your skeleton you would not be able to run, jump, or even stand up. Your bones work together as a system, along with your muscles. The bones and muscles move together to keep you active.

Think about all of the ways your body moves. Even if you just want to pick up a book or write your name, you are using bones and muscles.

Doctors and nurses know all of the names of the bones in your body. But there's no reason you can't know their names also. Study the diagram of the skeleton. Learn the names of the bones. It's a great way to find out more about your body. And if you ever plan to be a doctor or nurse one day, you'll already be on your way to learning!

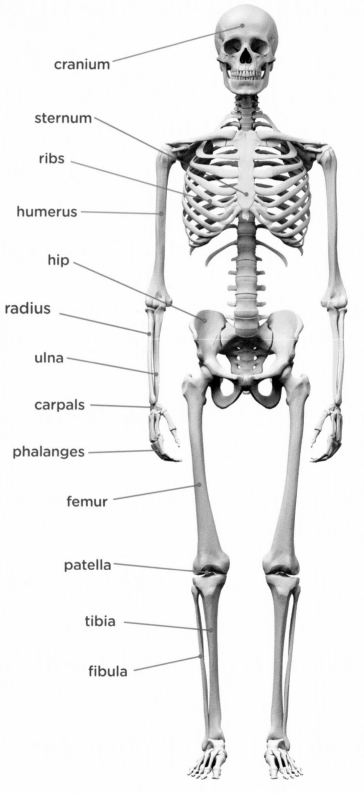

cranium

sternum

ribs

humerus

hip

radius

ulna

carpals

phalanges

femur

patella

tibia

fibula

Read each question and circle the correct answer. Then answer the questions below.

1. Which bone in your body protects your brain?

   a) carpals   b) cranium   c) tibia   d) sternum

2. Which bone is part of the arm?

   a) patella   b) tibia   c) fibula   d) humerus

3. Which bones move when you type on a computer?

   a) ribs   b) patella   c) phalanges   d) fibula

4. Which bone is NOT part of the leg?

   a) radius   b) tibia   c) femur   d) fibula

5. Which bone moves when you wave to someone?

   a) patella   b) cranium   c) ribs   d) radius

6. Which bone helps to protect your heart?

   a) ulna   b) sternum   c) carpals   d) tibia

7. Are your bones needed if you simply want to sit down in a chair? Why or why not?

   _____

8. Which other body system works together with your skeleton?

   _____

Tornado Alley

A tornado is a funnel of clouds and winds that forms during a large storm system. These winds can move quickly. They can be very dangerous. It is not hard to spot a tornado in the distance. A tornado looks like a cone rotating in the sky. The top of the tornado is wider than the bottom, near the ground. The area of a tornado that reaches the ground can be very small. But these storms pack a powerful punch wherever they touch land. Tornadoes have been known to form very quickly. They can also destroy buildings and other property. The strongest tornadoes can have winds that whip at more than 300 miles (483 km) per hour.

In the United States, tornadoes happen most frequently in one area. That region from Texas to South Dakota has become known as Tornado Alley. In the spring, warm, moist air blows north from the Gulf of Mexico. As it passes over the flat land, it meets dry air. That air comes from Canada and the Rocky Mountains. The two systems meet and cause many storms. Many of them create the swirling pattern needed for a tornado to form. The map shows the area that makes up Tornado Alley.

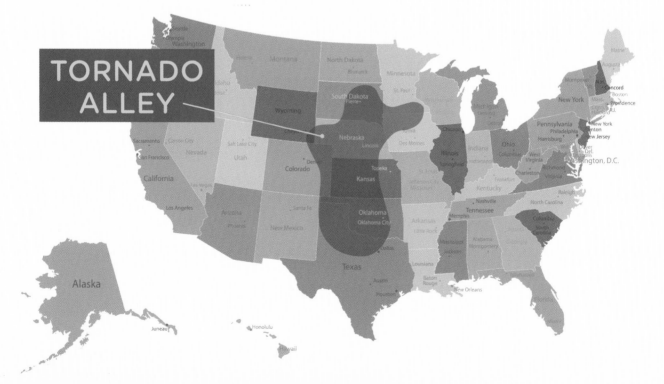

1. Which state is NOT part of Tornado Alley?

   a) Kansas   **b)** Oklahoma   **c)** Iowa   **d)** Arizona

2. What is the state located farthest east that is part of Tornado Alley?

   a) North Dakota   **b)** Wyoming   **c)** Iowa   **d)** Texas

3. Which area has the least impact on the number of tornadoes in Tornado Alley each year?

   a) Canada   **b)** Mexico   **c)** Gulf of Mexico   **d)** Rocky Mountains

4. Which of the following questions cannot be answered by examining the map?

   a) How many states are part of Tornado Alley?

   b) What causes tornadoes to form?

   c) What is the northern-most state that is part of Tornado Alley?

   d) Which major source of water is closest to Tornado Alley?

5. How many miles per hour are the winds of the strongest tornadoes?

   a) 50   **b)** 100   **c)** 300   **d)** 30,000

6. During which season do tornadoes occur most often?

   a) winter   **b)** spring   **c)** summer   **d)** fall

7. Summarize why the center of the United States is called Tornado Alley.

   _____

   _____

8. Which sentence from the passage describes the effects of tornadoes?

   _____

Baseball Through the Years

It's been called America's pastime. Baseball has been an important part of American history since before the start of the Civil War. People say a man named Abner Doubleday invented the sport in 1839 in Cooperstown, New York.

The first professional team, the Cincinnati Red Stockings, was formed in 1869, during the Civil War. By 1900, two baseball leagues had started—the National League and the American League. Today's modern teams still make up these two leagues. Teams in each league play each other until there is just one winning team. The winning teams in each league then face off at the end of the season in the World Series.

From the very beginning, the game of baseball quickly became known as a game that brought people together. Throughout the early 1900s, many baseball stadiums were built to house large crowds. It seemed that everyone wanted to go to games to see their local teams play. In 1921, baseball games began to be broadcast on the radio for people to hear.

Baseball even continued through two world wars. During World War II, however, 340 Major League baseball players and thousands of minor-league players served in the war. That meant that there were not enough players at home. That's when the All-American Girls Professional Baseball League was formed. The league played from 1943 through the end of the war, and stopped playing in 1954.

Today, the equipment and uniforms may look more modern. But the game is still played almost exactly the way it was during its very first games. America's pastime is bound to continue to entertain people for a long time to come.

Answer the questions.

1. When and where was the game of baseball invented?

_____

2. What was name of the first professional baseball team?

_____

3. How is it decided who plays in the World Series each year?

_____

_____

4. When were many large baseball stadiums built in the United States?

_____

5. How did baseball change in 1921?

_____

6. How did baseball change during World War II?

_____

_____

7. How are baseball games today different from the very first games?

_____

_____

8. How are baseball games today the same as the very first games?

_____

_____

Olympics: In the Beginning

What's the oldest sporting event in the world? Is it the World Series? Is it the Super Bowl? Maybe it's the New York City Marathon. Not even close! The Olympic Games were first held over 2,500 years ago.

The Olympic Games were first established in ancient Greece. They were meant to honor the Greek God, Zeus. The games were a huge event held every four years. Jugglers and other entertainers performed between events. There were giant barbeques for the crowds after the events were over. Legends were born from these ancient games. One involves a wrestler name Milo. He was said to have trained every day by carrying a calf on his shoulders. He became famous for his superhuman strength.

After the days of Ancient Greece, there were no more Olympic Games. It was not until 1896 that the first modern Olympic Games were started. These events were much closer to the ones we recognize today. For example, the first marathon was held during the 1896 games. Over the years, the Olympics became a celebration of sportsmanship around the world. With each game, more nations began to take part in the celebration. Today, around eighty-eight nations and about 2,800 athletes take part in the Olympics. The Summer Games and Winter Games occur at different locations. The city that hosts the event puts on a spectacular show to welcome the world to the games.

Athletes compete in fifty-six sports and about three hundred events. The gold, silver, and bronze medals are given to the first-, second-, and third-place winners in each event. Every two years, the world turns its attention to the centuries-old tradition of the Olympics. Olympic athletes will continue to make their countries proud well into the future.

Circle the best word or phrase to complete each sentence.

1. The oldest sporting event in history is the _____.

   Super Bowl   Olympics

2. The original Olympic Games were meant to honor _____.

   athletes   Zeus

3. The ancient wrestler Milo was said to have trained by _____ every day.

   running a marathon   carrying a calf

4. The modern Olympics that we know today were started _____.

   in 1896   about 3,000 years ago

5. Today's Olympics are a celebration of _____.

   sportsmanship   strength

6. Today about _____ nations take part in the Olympics.

   2,800   eighty-eight

7. Today there are about _____ sports to take part in during the Olympics.

   fifty-six   three hundred

8. During each Olympics, a different _____ welcomes people to the games.

   athlete   city

Bald Eagles

Imagine a bird with snowy-white feathers, supersharp claws, and wings that span longer than the height of a human. That bird is the bald eagle, the national bird of the United States.

The bird is found only in North America. It soars over lakes and rivers where it can find fish to eat. It swoops down on its prey and grabs it in its talons, or claws. The bird gets many of its meals, however, by stealing the prey caught by other animals.

In the early half of the 1900s, bald eagles were hunted in large numbers. The use of pesticides also affected the number of bald eagles. The pesticides got into rivers and lakes. They collected in fish. Then the eagles ate the fish. The poisons made the shells of eagle eggs very weak. Many of the birds never hatched because of the damaged eggs. The number of bald eagles dropped dramatically. The national bird was in danger of extinction.

But people helped to protect the bird. The use of the pesticide that harmed eagles was outlawed. Hunting was also not permitted. People helped to keep the bird safe. Over the years, this allowed the numbers of bald eagles to rise.

Today the bald eagle is no longer endangered. It has returned to many of the places it once roamed. Its huge nests can be seen high in trees. Eagle pairs help tend to their eggs each year. As each new baby eagle is born, our national bird continues to be an amazing success story.

The story of the bald eagle shows how we can learn from our mistakes. We are understanding the effects of our actions. And most importantly, we are learning how to fix our errors.

Read each statement. Write *true* or *false*. Then answer the questions below.

1. The bald eagle is the national bird of United States and Canada. _____

2. The bald eagle hunts for food over lakes and rivers. _____

3. The bald eagle steals food that other animals have caught. _____

4. Eagles catch fish from the water with their sharp beaks. _____

5. Bald eagles became endangered due to hunting and the use of pesticides. _____

6. Why were pesticides a problem for bald eagles?

_____

_____

7. How did humans help the bald eagle?

_____

_____

8. Why is the bald eagle considered a success story?

_____

_____

Constellations

Gazing up into the nighttime sky can take anyone by surprise. On a clear night, it seems as if distinct pictures are up in the sky, staring back at you. Stars light up the night in patterns called constellations. There are eighty-eight official constellations in the sky. These constellations have been named and can be traced in their journey across the sky each night and during each season.

While scientists today track stars with high-tech methods, constellations date back to ancient times. Records of pictures of the night sky date back 4,000 years. They may even go back further than any written records. People named the constellations after the pictures they felt were represented. The ancient Greeks named some of the constellations we know today.

The hunter, Orion, looks like a man wearing armor and shooting an arrow. The constellation called Leo looks like a lion in the sky. Of course, you have to use your imagination to see it exactly. Your eyes must fill in the gaps between the stars. Think of it like a connect-the-dots picture.

Constellations were useful in ancient times because they helped people to find their way. They helped sailors navigate at night. The constellations are always in the same spot during each season. So if you want to head north, you can quickly figure out which way to go based on the pictures in the sky.

Today, ships have complex navigation systems. They don't need to rely on constellations. But constellations still help us study the night sky. One of the easiest constellations to spot in the sky is the Big Dipper. Go out at night and take a look! You'll see what looks like a pot with a long handle. What other pictures do you see in the night sky?

Circle each true statement.

1. There are 4,000 constellations in the night sky.

2. A constellation is a pattern of stars in the sky.

3. Most constellations are made up of eighty-eight stars.

4. Constellations were discovered about 100 years ago.

5. The constellation Orion looks like a hunter wearing armor.

6. The constellation Leo looks like a bear.

7. People used to use constellations to find their way at night.

8. Ships today still rely on constellations to find their way.

Iditarod

"Mush!" That's the call of the official "mushers" of the Iditarod dogsled race. The race is named after a river in Alaska. The name means "distant place." This exciting, bone-chilling event happens each March in Alaska. Starting in Anchorage, each musher, or dogsled leader, starts with a team of sixteen dogs. The teams set off on a thousand-mile journey. They travel through forests, tundra, and other difficult, snowy terrain. The race ends in Nome, Alaska, when the last team crosses the finish line. The race is often referred to as the Last Race on Earth due to its challenges and remote location.

The race has become a symbol of hard work and determination. Both mushers and dogs must have strong bodies and minds to take part in the Iditarod.

The fastest winning time for the Iditarod was accomplished in 2014. That's when musher Dallas Seavey and his dog team finished the race in 8 days, 13 hours, 4 minutes, and 19 seconds.

There are rules in place to protect the mushers and dogs. Each team needs to rest a certain amount of time. Even with the rest, however, the race is very demanding. Mushers use different tactics to help them finish the race. They might feed their dogs at different times each day. Or they might only ride at a certain time of day. Each musher must start the race with all of the equipment he or she will need. That includes a heavy sleeping bag. It also includes food for themselves and the dogs and boots for all the dogs.

Check out the chart of records made by Iditarod mushers.

Musher	Record	Year
Dallas Seavey	Fastest Winning Time	2014
Rick Swenson	Most Times Won (5)	1977, 1979, 1981, 1982, 1991
Lance Mackey	Most Times Won in a Row (4)	2007, 2008, 2009, 2010
Dallas Seavey	Youngest Musher to Win	2012
Libby Riddles	First Female to Win	1985

Circle the correct word or phrase to complete each sentence.

1. An opinion about the Iditarod that was expressed in the passage is that it _____.

   starts in Anchorage   is exciting and bone-chilling

2. A fact about the Iditarod that was expressed in the passage is that _____.

   each team includes sixteen dogs   the race symbolizes hard work

3. The Iditarod race ends when _____.

   the first musher finishes   the last musher finishes

4. The musher with the fastest time completed the race in _____.

   2014   2012

5. The musher who won the most Iditarod races won _____ times.

   four   five

6. Mushers bring equipment on the dogsled with them, including food for _____.

   themselves only   themselves and the dogs

7. The youngest musher to ever win the Iditarod race was _____.

   Dallas Seavey   John Baker

8. Libby Riddles set an Iditarod record by being _____.

   the first female to race   the first female to win

Video Games

How far would you guess video games date back? The very first video game was actually made in the 1940s! At the World's Fair, inventor Edward Condon displayed a huge computer that used buttons and knobs to play a game called Nim, in which the person—playing against the computer—tries to avoid picking up the last matchstick. Video games—sometimes called simulations—were also used by the military after World War II.

By 1958, an electronic game called Tennis for Two was invented. Two people played against each other. They used separate controllers that connected to a computer. A simple dot moved back and forth across a screen like a game of tennis or Ping-Pong.

In 1980, Pac-Man was released. It was at this time that video games took off as a popular pasttime. Teenagers flocked to video game arcades to play the latest games. Each game cost a quarter to play. Teens spent hours playing games such as Asteroids and Donkey Kong.

In 1977, the first home video game system, the Atari 2600, had been released. This allowed people to enjoy games at home. In 1985, Nintendo entered the home video game market and has stayed in the game ever since. Each time a new system is released for home video games, the graphics, or look, of the games get better and better. Sony and Microsoft also compete to bring customers new systems and games.

In fact, the home video game industry is bigger than the movie industry and the music industry. With such incredible graphics in some of today's video games, it is becoming hard to tell a video game from a movie!

Read each question and circle the correct answer. Then answer the questions below.

1. When was the first video game invented?

   a) 1880s   b) 1940s   c) 1950s   d) 1980s

2. What was the object of the first video game?

   a) to play tennis   b) to race cars

   c) to shoot airplanes   d) to avoid picking up the last matchstick

3. When was the game Tennis for Two invented?

   a) 1880s   b) 1940s   c) 1950s   d) 1980s

4. Which video game first caused arcades to become popular in the 1980s?

   a) Donkey Kong   b) Pac-Man

   c) Tennis for Two   d) Asteroids

5. Which company was NOT mentioned as making home video game systems?

   a) Nintendo   b) Apple   c) Sony   d) Microsoft

6. According to the passage, what has been improved most throughout the history of video games?

   a) graphics   b) sound   c) price   d) complexity

7. Which sentence from the passage shows that video games are extremely popular today?

   _____

8. What does the author compare the graphics of a video game to?

   _____

The Popularity of Superheroes

Comic book heroes seem to be everywhere these days. Batman, Superman, Captain America, and Spider-Man all have big hit movies. One reason these superheroes are such big hits at the box office is because they were already popular for generations.

People pay high prices for old comic books. The very first Superman comic book sold for more than $3 million on eBay. It was the most expensive comic book ever sold. It was also one of the most expensive items to ever sell on eBay.

High-ticket sales at the box office are also proof that people enjoy superheroes. Their movies sell out quickly. People of all ages are buying the tickets. It's not just children. Families and older adults are enjoying these movies, too.

The most appealing thing about superheroes is likely their ability to defeat evil. Moviegoers look up to characters that can fight for those in need.

Most of the superheroes we watch on the big screen are based on comic books from the past. The Golden Age of Comics was during the 1940s. This was during World War II and the start of the Cold War. At that time, there was a large demand for stories of good against evil. Comic books filled that need. And the lightweight books were inexpensive and easy to carry, too.

Today people may enjoy these old stories because they are a reminder of those patriotic days. They may also enjoy the impressive special effects of today's movies. Whatever the reason people are interested in superheroes today, their movies will continue to be popular with young people for generations to come.

Read each statement. Write *fact* or *opinion*. Then answer the question below.

1. Superheroes were popular in the past. _____

2. Superheroes will continue to be popular in the future. _____

3. A high-priced comic book on eBay shows that many people like superheroes. _____

4. Good movie-ticket sales for superhero movies show that many people like superheroes. _____

5. The best comics came out in the 1940s. _____

6. Moviegoers look up to characters that fight evil. _____

7. People enjoy comic book heroes today because they remind them of the past. _____

8. Write your opinion about comic books.

_____

_____

Snowflakes

Snowflakes sure look pretty as they fall from the sky. But they are more than just pretty. They tell a story about what the weather is like at the moment they fall.

Each snowflake is a single ice crystal. A snowflake forms when a drop of water freezes onto a piece of dust or other particle high in the sky. Each ice crystal has six "arms" that extend out from the center.

Every snowflake has a different pattern. Some have long arms like needles. Others are flat like plates. Some arms look like tiny tree branches or leaves. The pattern is the same on the six arms of each snowflake.

What gives snowflakes these different shapes? It depends on the exact temperature and amount of moisture in the air as the snow falls. For example, at 23 degrees Fahrenheit (-5 degrees C), you will see ice crystals with long, needle-like arms. When it is as cold as 5 degrees Fahrenheit (-15 degrees C), crystals will be flatter. They will look more like plates.

A snowflake can change many times as it falls through the sky. As the flake falls, the temperature and conditions can change from second to second. Air near the ground may be warmer than air higher up. This affects the way each flake looks.

Each arm looks exactly the same because it is part of the same flake. Each arm experiences the same conditions as the others. But each individual snowflake is different from every other. That's because each flake takes a slightly different path through the air. One may blow in a different direction. It may go through warmer or cooler air than the one next to it. Each snowflake's unique path creates it individual shape!

Answer the questions.

1. How is a snowflake formed?

_____

2. Can you describe the shape that all snowflakes have in common?

_____

3. Why don't all snowflakes look alike?

_____

4. Which sentence from the passage explains why some snowflakes have arms that are long like needles?

_____

_____

5. Why can a snowflake change shape as it falls from the sky?

_____

_____

6. Why are the arms of each snowflake the same?

_____

7. Why is each snowflake different from all others?

_____

_____

8. What are some ways that air can be different in different places?

_____

Dr. Seuss on the Loose

Dr. Seuss is one of the most popular children's book writers. He has been for generations! What made Dr. Seuss special?

Theodor Seuss Geisel was born in 1904 in Massachusetts. To put Ted to bed at night, his mother chanted rhyming poems. The poems had always been fun for him to listen to. They influenced Ted's desire to write rhyming books when he grew older. They also helped to make him so good at it!

When Ted grew up, he became an illustrator. He also worked in advertising as an artist. But he had a tough time getting his first children's book published. The first book that he wrote and illustrated was called *And to Think That I Saw It on Mulberry Street*. It was turned down twenty-seven times before a publisher finally bought the book. It was published in 1937 under the name Dr. Seuss.

Soon after, Ted struck it big in the children's book world. He was asked to write a book that used only 225 words that new readers learn in school. It was meant to give kids a more interesting schoolbook. It was a new way to learn while having fun. It was a new idea for schoolbooks.

Ted's book, *The Cat in the Hat*, was a big hit. It was sold to schools. But it was also sold in bookstores. That's where the book became such a big hit. People have been buying *The Cat in the Hat* since 1957. It has become a favorite for many children learning to read.

Dr. Seuss wrote and illustrated forty-four books for kids. His lively rhymes made him an all-time favorite author of kids everywhere. What's your favorite Dr. Seuss book?

Answer the questions.

1. What is the passage about?

_____

2. Summarize the information in the second paragraph.

_____

_____

3. What jobs did Theodor Geisel do before becoming a children's book author?

_____

4. What was Dr. Seuss's first book?

_____

5. Summarize how Dr. Seuss came to write *The Cat in the Hat*.

_____

6. Name two different places where *The Cat in the Hat* was sold.

_____

7. Which sentence from the passage explains how long *The Cat in the Hat* has been a success?

_____

8. What is a question you have about Dr. Seuss's life? Where can you find the answer?

_____

_____

The Future Is Bright

Do people ever ask you what you want to be when you grow up? It's one of the toughest questions anyone has to answer. Even once you answer, you might change your mind a bunch of times as you grow up!

There are good reasons people get confused about what they want to be when they are grown. Sometimes people haven't thought about what they enjoy doing. When you do something that you enjoy, you are likely to be happier. That's why people called career counselors can help. They assist people in making decisions about what they want to be. Then they help people decide what kind of training or education they need for that job.

Career counselors start by giving people questionnaires. The questions get people thinking about their likes and dislikes. Then the counselors can talk about what kinds of jobs are right for different personalities. Fill out the following short questionnaire to think about what makes you happiest!

Name _____

Age _____

Do you like being with large groups of people or small groups? Check one.
❑ large groups   ❑ small groups

Would you prefer working outdoors or indoors? Check one.
❑ outdoors   ❑ indoors

Do you like to work with numbers, words, or both? Check one.
❑ numbers   ❑ words   ❑ both

If you could work right now, what would your dream job be?

_____

Why?

_____

_____

Answer the questions.

1. What is the questionnaire about?

_____

2. What does the questionnaire help people do?

_____

3. Who gives people the questionnaire?

_____

4. What is the next step after filling out the questionnaire?

_____

_____

5. Why do you think someone should answer the questions again when they are older?

_____

6. What are some possible careers for someone who likes to work with numbers?

_____

7. Why do you think the questionnaire asks people about their dream job?

_____

8. What is another possible question to ask someone to find out what he or she likes?

_____

The Golden Gate Bridge

The Golden Gate Bridge in San Francisco, California, is one of the world's most beautiful bridges. As far back as the 1860s, people saw a need for a way to easily cross the mouth of the San Francisco Bay. The bay made it difficult for people to move from one side of it to another.

People started demanding a bridge as wonderful as the city itself. An engineering student and journalist named James Wilkins came up with an early plan. But his ideas for the bridge were too expensive. Instead of scrapping the plan, other people pitched in. They looked around for less expensive ways to make the bridge a reality. The result was amazing.

The process of building the bridge helped the city. By the time work began, it was the middle of the Great Depression. It was a time when many people were out of work. The bridge project helped to give many people jobs. It helped the struggling economy of the city.

The project lasted until May of 1937. At the time, the bridge had the longest roadway of any bridge in the world. The bridge is lightweight and flexible, too. A suspension bridge gets support from cables that stretch out from tall towers. The cables are anchored into the ground on both sides of the bridge. Extra support cables connect to the roadway.

About 200,000 people walked across the bridge to celebrate its opening. The orange paint on the bridge makes it stand out beautifully against the blue water of the bay. It didn't take long for the bridge to symbolize the great city of San Francisco.

Read each statement. Write *fact* or *opinion*. Then answer the question below.

1. The Golden Gate Bridge is one of the most beautiful bridges in the world. _____

2. People wanted a way to cross the San Francisco Bay easily. _____

3. The bridge is as wonderful as the city itself. _____

4. The first plans for the bridge were too expensive. _____

5. The bridge-building process created many jobs. _____

6. The Golden Gate Bridge is a suspension bridge. _____

7. The orange paint on the bridge was a good choice of color. _____

8. Write your own opinion about bridges.

_____

_____

Jane Goodall

Not all scientists work in laboratories. Some work out in the wild. They observe the natural world and share with us what they've learned about life.

Born in London, England, in 1934, Jane Goodall was always interested in nature and wildlife. As a child, she observed birds and other animals. She made notes and sketches about what she saw. Goodall read as much about animals and nature as she could. She dreamed of going to Africa to observe animals in their natural habitats.

In 1960, Goodall finally got her wish. After working with a scientist named Louis Leakey, Goodall got involved in research of chimpanzees. Goodall went to an area of Africa now known as Tanzania. After two years, the chimpanzees became comfortable with Goodall.

Jane's observations of chimps continued for decades. She saw the chimps using long stems of grass as tools. They dipped the stem into termite mounds. Then they raised the grass and ate the termite-covered grass. This was the first observation that an animal other than humans could use tools. She later observed the chimps using rocks, branches, and leaves. They used these simple tools to feed and clean themselves and as weapons.

Today, Jane Goodall spends a lot of her time traveling to educate people about the loss of animal habitats. Her work has brought people's attention to the intelligence of the chimps in Africa. It has made people aware that these animals need protection from humans. Hunting and building have made their habitats difficult to live in.

Goodall has learned how these animals live by living among them. Her work has helped inspire many other scientists to observe what is right before us in nature.

What's the order? Write *1, 2, 3, 4, 5, 6* on the lines. Then answer the questions below.

_____ Goodall started working with the scientist Louis Leakey.

_____ Goodall started living in Africa to observe chimpanzees.

_____ Goodall observed chimpanzees in Africa using tools.

_____ Goodall wrote about and sketched animals near her home.

_____ Goodall travels to educate people about animal habitats.

_____ Goodall was born in London, England.

1. Describe what Jane Goodall observed chimpanzees doing that showed that they are like humans.

_____

_____

2. Which sentence in the second paragraph shows that Jane had a childhood dream that eventually came true?

_____

_____

Jellyfish

Jellyfish are one of the oddest-looking creatures of the sea. They differ so much in the way they look, but all jellyfish are invertebrates. That means that they have no backbone. In fact, they have no bones in their bodies at all. A jellyfish's bell-shaped body is soft and squishy. But don't touch one if you come across it in the ocean. Some jellyfish have dangerous, poisonous stings.

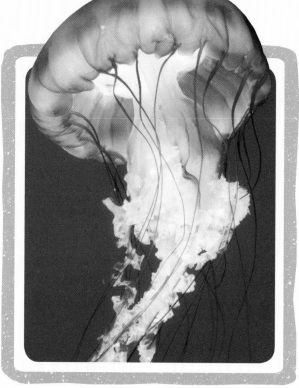

The parts of a jellyfish that extend below it are called tentacles. The tentacles are long and flexible arms that extend out from the animal. Many jellyfish have tiny body parts called cells that sting anything they touch. This is how the animal catches its food. It stings an animal that touches it. This often paralyzes the animal so that it cannot move. It then pulls the prey into the mouth found at the bottom of its body. Jellyfish digest, or break down, their food quickly. This allows them to keep floating with no problem. They eat shrimp, fish, and crabs.

Jellyfish sometimes sting humans, but it often happens by accident. A person might rub up against one in the water without realizing it. But jellyfish stings can be very painful. Some can even kill a person because of the poison in their tentacles.

In order to "swim" though the water, jellyfish squirt water from their mouths. That pushes their bodies forward through the water. Jellyfish are found in all areas of the ocean. They can be found in waters that are cold, warm, deep, or shallow. Some come in vibrant colors. Some jellyfish are even clear. Others give off a substance from their bodies that make them look as if they glow.

Draw a line to match each word from the passage to its meaning. Then answer the questions below.

1. invertebrate

a. to put an animal in a state in which it cannot move

2. tentacles

b. to break down food so that the body can use it for energy

3. cells

c. long, flexible arms of an invertebrate animal such as a jellyfish

4. paralyze

d. an animal with no backbone

5. poisonous

e. able to cause illness or death

6. digest

f. tiny body parts on a jellyfish's tentacles that sting anything they touch

7. How do jellyfish capture and eat their prey?

_____

_____

8. Why do jellyfish digest their food so quickly?

_____

_____

Answer Key

Answers to some of the pages may vary.

Page 5
1. Jupiter
2. solid rock
3. magnetic field
4. many
5. storms
6. hundreds of years
7. on its moons
8. oceans

Page 7
1. false
2. false
3. true
4. true
5. true
6. true
7. true
8. false

Page 9
1. America accepts immigrants from all around the world.
2. It is located in New York Harbor and was in operation from 1892 to 1954.
3. The author explains what the island meant to the people who came here and are now American citizens. This sentence is underlined: "It is a reminder of the struggle of immigrants who arrived in the country generations ago and made a new life."
4. Records included the name, age, and country of origin of every person who arrived. They also included physical exams.
5. Most came from Europe.
6. The Statue of Liberty stands for freedom and the opportunities that America offers.
7. It stands for the courage of immigrants who arrived in America looking for a new life.
8. Ellis Island is a reminder of a period in American history when immigrants used the island as a processing center to enter the country.

Page 11
1. cool off
2. sweat glands
3. mother
4. 700
5. plants, fruits, and small animals
6. smell
7. leather
8. more

Page 13
1. d
2. b
3. b
4. c
5. a
6. New safety features can save lives and keep people safer.
7. He found problems that needed to be solved and then tried to find a solution, just like inventors of today.
8. They try to find ways to solve things and make life easier for us.

Page 15
1. e
2. a
3. d
4. g
5. b
6. c
7. f
8. Answers will vary but may include the following: The International Space Station, or ISS, is a research laboratory in space that is operated by scientists from many different countries. They keep the station operating and live there while learning more about outer space.

Page 17
1. They are called fossils.
2. They lived 65 million years ago.
3. They looked at the shape of tooth fossils.
4. They had pointy, sharp teeth.
5. They had flat teeth for grinding and tearing leaves.
6. They can tell what dinosaurs looked like.
7. Answers will vary but may include: how they cared for young, how long they lived, and the color of their body coverings.
8. Answers will vary.

Page 19
1. d
2. e
3. a
4. c
5. b
6. Baby giraffes can be so big that they are even taller than a full-grown human.
7. They can go for even longer amounts of time without drinking water.
8. They run quickly from predators.

Page 21
1. 6, 4, 1, 5, 2, 3
2. She entered a race that she was not allowed in, brought attention to the problem, and helped to change unfair rules at the marathon.
3. Today, thousands of women run in marathons all around the world.

Page 23
The following true statements are circled: 2, 5, and 7.

Page 25
1. c
2. a
3. e
4. b
5. d
6. A lot of gold was found in California in 1848, and a lot of people rushed there to mine the gold and get rich. Boomtowns started, and some people made a lot of money. When the gold ran out, people left just as quickly as they arrived.
7. People used special pans to collect silt, gold, and water from the river. The water was swirled to let the silt and gold settle in the bottom of the pans and the gold was collected and sold.
8. The supply of gold ran out and people could no longer find enough to get rich.

Page 27
1. heart
2. coordination
3. brain
4. speed
5. pedaling
6. disease
7. outdoors
8. gasoline

Page 29
1. d
2. a
3. b
4. c
5. b
6. c
7. c
8. b

Page 31
1. d
2. b
3. a
4. c
5. a
6. c
7. c
8. a

Page 33
1. true
2. true
3. false
4. true
5. false
6. false
7. true
8. He used to take apart and assemble electronics with his father, which helped him learn about how electronics worked.

Page 35
1. It was made into a national park in 1872.
2. An underground supervolcano makes the area unique.
3. A geyser is a hot, underground spring that shoots a tall stream of water and steam high into the air.
4. Old Faithful erupts about every 90 minutes, and Steamboat Springs is the world's tallest geyser.
5. The supervolcano heats the underground features in the area.
6. In 1883, railroads were built to help people get to Yellowstone.
7. In 1915, cars were allowed into the park for the first time.
8. Visitors can watch Old Faithful, hike, swim, and enjoy the scenery.

Page 37
1. mammal
2. birds
3. caves
4. sound
5. small insects
6. polar
7. endangered
8. increased

Page 39

1. The tusk is a long, sword-like horn that is really a tooth that sticks out of the upper jaw of male narwhals.
2. The narwhal tusk makes it look like a unicorn.
3. Narwhals eat shrimp, squid, and many types of fish.
4. Narwhals live in Arctic waters, so tropical waters would be too warm for the narwhal.
5. Russia and Greenland
6. They travel in groups of ten to a hundred, called pods.
7. They are mammals, so they need to come to the surface occasionally to breathe.
8. They are hunted by polar bears and orcas, and their habitats are threatened by climate change.

Page 41

1. opinion
2. fact
3. fact
4. fact
5. opinion
6. fact
7. opinion
8. Answers will vary.

Page 43

1. c
2. c
3. d
4. a
5. d
6. b
7. As a child, she enjoyed many of the same activities that Girl Scouts do.
8. She was deaf and she felt it was important that the Girl Scouts welcomed members with disabilities.

Page 45

1. rules
2. voting for one person
3. it can be difficult
4. hang posters
5. interesting
6. responsible
7. make your ideas known
8. work well with others

Page 47

1. When people go camping, they should show respect for nature by not leaving a trace that they were there.
2. Remove all traces of food or packaging that is brought into a campsite.
3. Use campsites that have already been cleared, and don't dig holes or ditches in the ground.
4. It can introduce new seeds or insects that are in the wood, which can change the environment.
5. Don't feed the animals you see.
6. Campfires should not be left unattended because they can cause forest fires. Millions of forest acres are burned each year, and they move about 14 miles (22.5 km) per hour as they damage everything in their path.
7. Everyone should be able to enjoy the quiet beauty of nature when they are camping.
8. The passage gives tips about how to go camping without leaving a trace or damaging the environment.

Page 49

Answers will vary but may include:
1. good hearing and eyesight; can twist its head more than halfway around; stiff feathers
2. great vision; eats both plants and animals
3. sprays predators with strong-smelling oil that keeps predators away; can be recognized easily by its white stripe
4. female carries young in a pouch; only pouched animal in North America; plays dead to trick predators

Page 51

4, 2, 6, 1, 5, 3, 7
Answers will vary but should include two of the following: knife, brush for olive oil, baking sheet, oven, oven mitt, or bowl for marinara sauce.

Page 53

1. false
2. false
3. false
4. true
5. true
6. Answers will vary but may include: receiving a gift, attending a party, providing help setting up a party, spending time, or surprising someone.
7. Thanking someone shows that you understand the effort that person made for you and what he or she did to help you.
8. To show that the sender is a good friend who can be counted on.

Page 55

1. e
2. b
3. a
4. c
5. d
6. Technology is changing quickly, which has good and bad effects on the world. More hackers are stealing identities online. But technologies such as virtual reality are helping people train safely for dangerous jobs.
7. People must be more protected from hackers.
8. The device can allow the soldier to experience a different scene and react to it safely.

Page 57

1. opinion
2. fact
3. fact
4. fact
5. opinion
6. I think
7. paragraph 3
8. Answers will vary.

Page 59

1. c
2. b
3. d
4. a
5. b
6. a
7. The smoothie contains as much spinach and cucumber as you would eat during a meal.
8. It is described as delicious, and the vegetables are described as sweeter when mixed with fruits.

Page 61

1. c
2. a
3. e
4. d
5. b
6. Some snakes, such as the garter snake, are harmless. Others, like the king cobra, are dangerous.
7. They can use a poison made in their bodies, called venom. They can also constrict their prey by squeezing it tightly.
8. It can unhinge its jaw to fit a larger animal in its mouth.

Page 63

1. false
2. false
3. true
4. true
5. true
6. The referee makes sure players follow the rules and decides when a foul has been made.
7. The goalie guards the team's goal and prevents the ball from being kicked into the goal by the opposite team.
8. The best way to play soccer is to have fun and play fair.

Page 65

1. b
2. d
3. c
4. a
5. d
6. b
7. Yes, bones are needed for any movement of the body.
8. The muscles work with your skeleton.

Page 67

1. d
2. c
3. b
4. b
5. c
6. b
7. Warm, moist air blowing north from the Gulf of Mexico meets dry air blowing south from Canada and the Rocky Mountains. The air creates storms.
8. They can also destroy buildings and other property.

Page 69
1. The game was said to be invented in 1839 in Cooperstown, New York.
2. The first team was the Cincinnati Red Stockings.
3. The winners of the National League and American League play each other in the World Series.
4. Many stadiums were built in the early 1900s.
5. In 1921, baseball was broadcast on the radio for the first time.
6. About 340 Major League baseball players and thousands of minor-league players served in the war. The All-American Girls Professional Baseball League was formed.
7. The uniforms and equipment are more modern than in the past.
8. The rules of the game are very similar to the ones played in the first game.

Page 71
1. Olympics
2. Zeus
3. carrying a calf
4. in 1896
5. sportsmanship
6. eighty-eight
7. fifty-six
8. city

Page 73
1. false
2. true
3. true
4. false
5. true
6. After eating contaminated fish, the eagle's eggs became too soft to survive.
7. People outlawed the pesticide that harmed the eagles, changed hunting laws, and protected the animals from harm.

8. People were successful in helping increase the number of bald eagles and getting them removed from the endangered list.

Page 75
The following true statements are circled: 2, 5, and 7.

Page 77
1. is exciting and bone chilling
2. each team includes sixteen dogs
3. the last musher finishes
4. 2014
5. five
6. themselves and the dogs
7. Dallas Seavey
8. the first female to win

Page 79
1. b
2. d
3. c
4. b
5. b
6. a
7. In fact, the home video game industry is bigger than the movie industry and the music industry.
8. a movie

Page 81
1. fact
2. opinion
3. opinion
4. fact
5. opinion
6. opinion
7. opinion
8. Answers will vary.

Page 83
1. Water droplets freeze onto dust or other particles in the sky and become ice crystals.
2. All snowflakes have six arms that extend out from the center.
3. The temperature and air conditions affect the way each snowflake looks.

4. For example, at 23 degrees Fahrenheit (-5 degrees C), you will see ice crystals with long, needle-like arms.
5. The temperature and air conditions are different in different places, and they can change each second. The snowflake changes according to these conditions.
6. All six arms are part of the same snowflake, so they took the same path through the air.
7. Each snowflake takes a different path through the sky, even if it is only slightly different. This makes the shape of each snowflake unique.
8. Temperature and moisture can change in different places through the sky.

Page 85
1. The passage is about the life of Theodor Geisel, the author who wrote books as Dr. Seuss.
2. Ted Geisel's mother used to chant rhymes to him as he went to bed as a child. This influenced his desire to write rhymes when he got older.
3. He was an illustrator and advertising artist.
4. *And to Think That I Saw It on Mulberry Street*
5. He was asked to write a book that included 225 words that new readers learned in school.
6. *The Cat in the Hat* was sold to schools and also sold in bookstores.
7. People have been buying *The Cat in the Hat* since 1957.
8. Answers will vary.

Page 87
1. It's about a person's likes and dislikes.
2. It helps people decide what kind of career might be best for them.
3. A career counselor gives the questionnaire.
4. The next step is talking to the career counselor about

possible careers and the education or training that would be needed.
5. A person's likes and dislikes might change over the years.
6. Answers will vary but may include math teacher, scientist, or accountant.
7. It makes people think about what they might enjoy.
8. Answers will vary.

Page 89
1. opinion
2. fact
3. opinion
4. fact
5. fact
6. fact
7. opinion
8. Answers will vary.

Page 91
3, 4, 5, 2, 6, 1
1. She observed them using tools to do things. For example, they used long grass to get termites out of a mound, and they used plants and rocks as tools.
2. She dreamed of going to Africa to observe animals in their natural habitats.

Page 93
1. d
2. c
3. f
4. a
5. e
6. b
7. They use their tentacles to sting, poison, and paralyze their prey. Then they pull them into their mouth.
8. Jellyfish digest their food quickly so they can keep floating.

Image Credits